Cut out the pages. Staple them to make a mini-book.

Meet Shinrai

1

This is Shinrai the camel.
Shinrai is trustworthy.

This means Shinrai does what she says she will do.

3

Shinrai is a good friend.
She is loyal and true.

4

Shinrai is honest and does not cheat.

Parent: Explain to your child that you want him or her to be a trustworthy person. Talk together about the different pictures. Explain that returning library books on time shows that you keep your word, giving gifts is one way to be a loyal friend, and not keeping something that is not yours shows honesty.

Learning About Trustworthiness

Meet Shinrai!

Shinrai is the camel who represents the character trait of trustworthiness. Her name is from the Japanese word for "trust." Shinrai is the kind of friend everyone wants because she does what she says she'll do, is loyal and true, and looks out for her friends. Shinrai can be counted on to stand up for what's right, no matter what others think.

Ideas for Teaching Trustworthiness at Home

One of the most important challenges parents face is to help our children develop strong characters based on good values. Here are a few simple ideas to start with:

1. Use the word *trustworthy* as you do each activity page with your child. This way your child will become familiar with the concept and will absorb the word into his or her vocabulary. Talk often about being trustworthy, using examples from your own life and the news.

2. Tell your child that you want him or her to be trustworthy. You expect it. Reward trustworthy behavior and discourage behavior that is not trustworthy. If you notice your child, yourself, or others acting trustworthy, point this out to your child. Talk about who's being trustworthy. Talk about the probable consequences of the behavior.

3. Help your child understand that trustworthy behavior is essential to building meaningful relationships with family, friends, classmates, and co-workers. Give appropriate examples from your own life of how trust has strengthened relationships, or how a lack of trust or a betrayal of trust has damaged relationships.

4. Be careful and conscious about setting a good example of being trustworthy in everything you do and say. What you do and don't do sends a message to your child.

What Will Shinrai Teach?

Here are some concepts about trustworthiness that Shinrai will help your child understand:

People who are trustworthy . . .

- stand up for their beliefs
- pursue goals with perseverance
- are honest in their words and deeds
- keep promises
- are reliable
- are loyal to friends, family, school, country

Using the T.E.A.M. Strategy

The T.E.A.M. strategy, developed by the CHARACTER COUNTS℠ Coalition is an effective approach for developing character.

TEACH
Teach your child that his or her character counts—that personal success and happiness will depend on who your child is on the inside, not on what he or she has or how he or she looks.

ENFORCE
Reward your child's good behavior and discourage all instances of bad behavior by imposing fair, consistent consequences that prove you are serious about character.

ADVOCATE
Be an advocate for character. Don't be neutral about the importance of character nor casual about improper conduct.

MODEL
Be careful and self-conscious about setting a good example in everything you say and do. Everything you do, and don't do sends a message about your values.

Remember, the development of good character is a process. You are building character a day at a time and often the path is two steps forward and one step back. The ongoing efforts you make will be rewarded as your child becomes a person of good character!

Who Is It?

Connect the dots from **A** to **Z**.

Parent: This page introduces Shinrai the camel, who represents trustworthiness. Explain to your child that Shinrai has earned the medal of character because she is trustworthy. Ask your child what it means to trust someone. Talk about positive and negative examples from your child's own experience. Then ask, *Which of these two statements do you want people to be able to say to you— "I trust you" or "I don't trust you"?*

Do What You Say You'll Do

Listen to each story. Which picture shows someone who keeps his or her word? Circle that picture.

Parent: Remind your child that a trustworthy person keeps his or her word. Whether talking to friends, family, or strangers, when a trustworthy person says he or she will do something, it gets done. Model keeping your word to your child by avoiding making commitments to him or her that you are unable to keep. Children need to know that adults will follow through on what they say.

Shinrai's Busy Day

Shinrai is always on time!
Draw a line to the matching clock for each appointment.

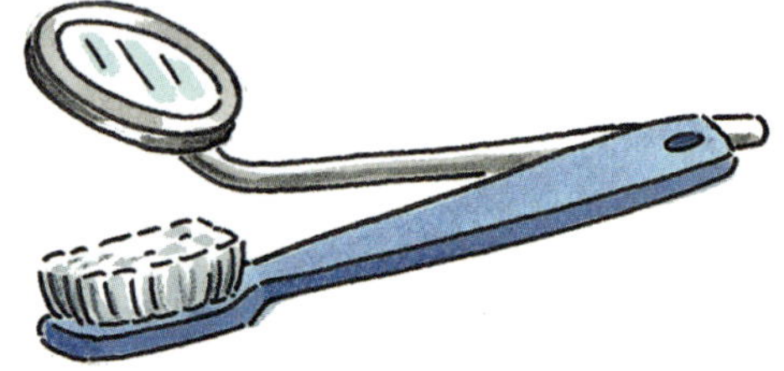

Shinrai has to be at the dentist at 9:00 in the morning.

Shinrai is meeting Austus for lunch at 1:00 in the afternoon.

Shinrai has soccer practice at 4:00 in the afternoon.

Time for bed! Shinrai is going to sleep at 8:00 at night.

Parent: Discuss the value of being on time for appointments. Explain that when a person is on time, it shows reliability, and respect for the person with whom he or she has the appointment.

What Should Ben Do?

Help Ben have the courage to do the right thing.
Circle the picture that shows the trustworthy thing to do.

Ben breaks a dish.

Ben hides it.

Ben tells his mom.

Ben finds a dollar.

Ben takes it to the Lost and Found.

Ben buys candy.

Ben has homework.

Ben watches TV.

Ben does his homework.

Parent: Help your child understand which choices show that Ben is trustworthy. Trustworthy people tell others what they need to know, do not keep what is not theirs, and do what they are supposed to do.

Who's a Good Friend?

Listen to the story and each question.
Answer the question aloud.
Trace the question mark.

Why is it wrong to play in the old house?

Who is standing up for right?

Who is a loyal friend?

Parent: Talk with your child about the answers to each question. Help your child understand that it is wrong to play in the old house because it is private property and because someone could get hurt. Explain to your child that sometimes he or she will need to have the courage to do what is right. This is hard when friends want to do something wrong, but you expect your child to do the right thing. Then talk about who the good friend is. Remind your child that good friends don't ask one another to do wrong things.

True Friend Mystery Picture

Who is hiding in the picture?

true—brown **loyal—green**

loyal true loyal loyal true true loyal true loyal true true true loyal true true loyal loyal true loyal loyal loyal loyal loyal loyal

Parent: Talk with your child about the meanings of the words *true* and *loyal*. Explain that untruthfulness involves more than just telling lies. It also includes saying you'll do something you cannot or will not do; exaggerating to make yourself look good or someone else look bad; and concealing information that someone needs to know. Loyalty is standing by your family, friends, school, and country.

If I Do This, Then . . .

Draw a line from each cause to the matching effect.

Cause

Effect

Parent: Help your child recognize what is going on in each picture. Explain that a trustworthy person does what he or she is supposed to do, even when no one else is looking.

Being Trustworthy

Look at the pictures. Read the words.
Circle the ways to be trustworthy.

Parent: Talk with your child about situations that are a normal part of his or her life and how to be trustworthy in those situations. Give examples from your own life as well, telling about times when you are truthful, do what you are supposed to do, and so on.

Keeping a Promise

Listen to the story.

Mrs. Lee said, "Will you walk my dog?"
Jen said, "I will walk your dog at 2:00."
At 2:00, Jen went to Mrs. Lee's house.
Jill saw her. Jill said, "Let's ride bikes."
Jen said, "I cannot play now."
"I promised to help Mrs. Lee."

Draw lines to complete each sentence.

Mrs. Lee said, "Will you walk my ______?"

2:00

Jen said, "I will walk your dog at ______.

Mrs. Lee

At 2:00, Jen went to Mrs. Lee's______."

bikes

Jill saw her. Jill said, "Let's ride______."

dog

Jen said, "I cannot play now.
I promised to help ______."

house

Parent: Remind your child that trustworthy people do what they say they will do. Make sure your child understands that sometimes people promise to do something and then change their minds. This is usually because keeping the promise has a cost that they had not anticipated. In this case the cost to Jen is missing out on bike riding with Jill. But your child should also understand that there is a cost to saying one thing and doing another. Encourage your child to be careful about making promises he or she cannot keep.

Missing Lunch

Mandy made a picnic lunch for her friends.
But they were late for the picnic! Mandy went to play.
While she was gone, the ants carried the food away.

Can you help the friends find the food?

Parent: This humorous page makes the point that there are usually consequences to being late. Talk with your child about some such consequences, including the loss of reputation, missing a flight or train, interrupting a meeting that has started, making others feel that they are unimportant, making others angry, and so on. Model being on time and help your child learn to be on time, too.

Find the Words

You have learned many new things since you were born. You will learn many more new things. Some things are hard to learn. But don't give up. Keep trying!

Find and circle the words.
The words go across and down.

Word Box

learn
try
new
hard
easy

g	h	e	a	s	y
r	a	s	t	n	s
t	r	k	e	e	t
b	d	m	y	w	r
l	e	a	r	n	y

Parent: Trustworthy people have integrity. One aspect of integrity is having the courage to try new things, even when they are hard or failure is a possibility. Tell your child that you want him or her to be willing to try new things occasionally. Give examples from your own life of both positive and negative experiences you have had trying new things. Explain to your child that trying new things is a part of growing, and that no one can be perfect at everything all the time. Trying is what's important.

Jeff Learns to Ride

Listen to the story. Cut out the pictures.
Paste them in order.

It was Jeff's birthday.
He got a two-wheeler bicycle.
He was afraid of falling.
His dad helped him learn to ride.
Soon Jeff could ride without help!

1	2	3

Parent: Some children need help to face new experiences with courage. Let your child know that you have confidence in him or her, and that failure is part of the process of growing and learning. Make sure you praise your child for his or her efforts, even if the results are not what was hoped for. This will help strengthen your child's resolve to try new things.

Shinrai Says Be Honest

Cut out, match, and paste to see what Shinrai says.

Be real about who you are.

Tell the truth.

Follow all rules and laws.

Tell lies so you won't get in trouble.

Parent: Explain to your child that you expect him or her to be honest. Honesty is important in both what we say and how we behave. Talk with your child about how to be honest in what he or she says—tell the truth, be real about who you are, and tell people things they would want to know. Help your child understand that honest actions include playing by the rules, not cheating, and not stealing.

Return What You Borrow

Shinrai borrowed a ball from Karina. Find a path to help Shinrai return the ball to Karina.

Parent: Trustworthy people take responsibilty for what they borrow and return borrowed items promptly. Work with your child to establish policies about borrowing from family members and from friends. Explain to your child that borrowing is risky because a borrower is responsible if an item is broken while he or she is using it. Ask your child *Would you want to loan your toys to someone who breaks them or who never brings them back? Why not?* Help your child understand that borrowing is a privilege which must be earned and can be lost.

You Be the Judge

Look at each picture.
Does the picture show someone being trustworthy?
Circle **yes** if it does. Circle **no** if it does not.

yes no

yes no

yes no

yes no

Parent: Look at each picture with your child and talk about what is happening. Talk together about the positive or negative consequences of each action being shown here.

Being Trustworthy

Choose the best title for each picture.
Write the title on the line.

Telling the Truth

A Fun Time

A Broken Promise

A Job Well Done

Parent: Talk with your child about the first picture. Explain that accidents such as ripping the book happen, but the boy did the right thing when he told his friend the truth. Talk about the second picture and ask your child if he or she has ever been in a situation like that. Remind your child that trustworthy people do what they are supposed to do, even when no one is watching.

Look Out for Others

Listen to each story. Which picture shows someone who looks out for others? Circle that picture.

Bella falls off her bike.

Isaac helps her up.

Isaac calls Bella a baby.

Mom has a bad cold.

Sam plays quietly.

Sam plays his drum.

Isaac can't find his favorite toy.

Bella helps him look for it.

Bella laughs at Isaac.

Parent: Trustworthy people are good friends and look out for those who care for them. Talk with your child about ways he or she can be a good friend and caring family member.

Be Loyal

Trustworthy people are loyal.
They stand up for and protect these groups.
Draw lines to match.

family

school

friends

country

Parent: Talk with your child about how you are loyal to your family, friends, and country. Then talk about how your child can be loyal to the groups shown.

I Can Be Trustworthy

Write your name on each line.

______________________________ can do the right thing.

______________________________ can be honest.

______________________________ can keep promises.

______________________________ can be loyal.

Color the gold medal of trustworthiness.
Draw a picture of yourself wearing it.

Parent: Let your child complete this page and post it in the bedroom or kitchen. Occasionally reread this page with your child and talk together about the importance of trustworthiness.